I0438010

Just Another Autistic Kid, But This One's Mine

A Journey Through Autism

Heidi Pfalzgraf

authorHOUSE®

AuthorHouse™
1663 Liberty Drive, Suite 200
Bloomington, IN 47403
www.authorhouse.com
Phone: 1-800-839-8640

First published by AuthorHouse   2/12/2009

ISBN: 978-1-4389-3743-4 (sc)

Printed in the United States of America
Bloomington, Indiana

This book is printed on acid-free paper.

For Kansas

Acknowledgements

I am sending out a sincere thank you to every angel listed below. You have either benefited us as a family or Kansas as an individual and we will always sing your praises. God bless you all.

Tiffany Baker
Allison Boggs
Rhonda Boughner
Connie Brady
Stephanie Brown
Dale & Joan Christman
Darren Cook
Dawn Crooks
Charles Denunzio Jr. DO
Shelby Falkenstein
Samantha Farnesworth PAC
Micah Fuchs
Danielle Greenlee & Family
Terrie Isaly
Lea Ladiga
Tanis Langsdorf
Lewisville Church of Christ
Crystal Longwell
Stacey Lucas
Marietta Memorial Pediatric
   Therapy Unit
Kari Marx
Carol Marmie & Family
Noel McFarland
Mellott Ridge Chruch of Christ

Susan Moore
Jacci Morgan
Rachel Perkins
Jack & Shirley Pfalzgraf
Windi Piatt
Jonathan Pittman
Shirley Pittman
Mary Rieck
Cindy Robertson
Gary & Patricia Rossiter
Paige Saling
Tabitha Saling
Tracy Saling
Megan Sherman
Courtney Smith
Tina Stahl
Angie Stimpert
Kristie Turner
Jennifer Weckbacher
Stacey Werkau
Jennifer Westfall
Savannah Yoho
Connie Young
Jackie Zinc

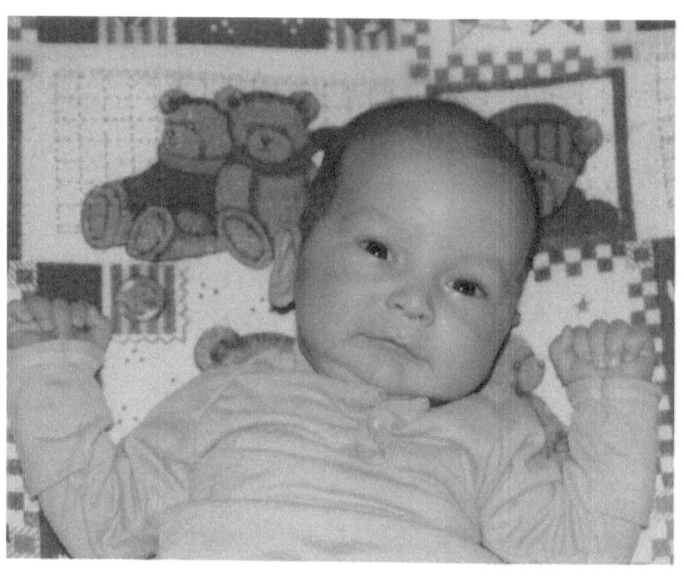

The Birth.

The excitement of having a boy was almost too much to bear. Our little girl was two and she brought such great joy to our lives. Now we were going to experience the best of both worlds.

My pregnancy was great. No morning sickness and the only complaints I had was that I felt extremely tired plus I gained a hefty 55 lbs.

He arrived on January 24th, 2002. My due date was 3 weeks away but my water broke in the middle of the night as I was taking my daughter to the potty. I felt a sharp pain and then a big relaxation of my stomach. I went to the bathroom and noticed slow drainage. I knew right away because my water had broke with my first child too. My first pregnancy ended in an emergency c-section because I would not dilate. I had already made plans for this one to be c-section as well. We made all necessary calls and headed for the hospital.

It was freezing outside and I kept thinking about how I hated to take a newborn out in the cold weather. We got to the hospital in the early morning and was told that my doctor wouldn't be in till after noon. We got comfortable and I started eating ice chips for breakfast. I had no pain and no dilation which was again exactly what happened with my first experience of labor.

The doctor showed up early about 10:00am and we all got suited up for surgery. I was given a spinal for numbness and I knew right away something was wrong. I was laying on my side and I was ready for the pain of the needle which is to be expected but it was more extreme than I could have ever imagined. I felt electric currents move down my back and into my legs. I screamed and the nurse grabbed the anesthesiologists hand. She actually said, "Something is not right!" But he just mouthed something back so I could not hear but she could read his lips and then he proceeded to repeat this action 3 more times. I truly believe I then went into shock because I could not talk or even move a facial muscle. It was and still is the scariest moment of my life, referring to my own body.

The surgery did not take very long and all of a sudden there was our baby boy. He was beautiful. His complexion was perfect. He came out so quiet that it alarmed me. I asked why he wasn't crying and the nurses just said he was looking around. Checking out the place. I brushed it off as believing he was just going to be a very content, easy-going baby. As soon as they started bathing him he began to cry. He cried until they laid him in my arms and then he stopped immediately. I thought, "Wow, he already knows his mama!" My love had enveloped this child unconditionally. My husband and I were so proud.

We named him Kansas. My husband is a school teacher and wants his children to have unusual names so they will be the only one with that name. We talked about changing our minds on the way to the hospital but decided to stay with Kansas. I knew when I saw his little face, he was definitely a Kansas. To this day, no one in our area has the same name.

Shortly after the excitement dwindled I demanded to speak with the anesthesiologist. He comes in and immediately started apologizing. I asked exactly what happened and he says that he put my spinal down the wrong channel and since he had already started he had to finish. I was so upset and asked if it was going to cause any side affects. He promised me it would not. It was just human error but nothing to be alarmed with. By the next day I was experiencing a headache. It was horrible while I was sitting up but immediately went away when I laid down. I was told by a nurse that I was having a spinal headache and it would eventually go away. It lasted the entire 4 days that I was there and I could not wait to go home. I had numbness in my right leg from my hip down to my knee for five months. I would definitely consider those side effects.

I was packing up the last bit of our stuff when the pediatrician comes in to my room and says, "Mrs. Pfalzgraf, Kansas has blood in his stool and we are going to have to keep him one more night so that we can run some tests." My emotions were of course out of sorts and I felt my eyes tear up within seconds. My perfect boy wasn't perfect?

We stayed another 24 hours and they ran every test they could, (so "they" said), plus changed his formula a few times. We were discharged with no answers as to why the blood was present and he was now using the most expensive formula on the market. We could see small traces of blood in Kansas' stool for the first 2 months of his life and was told by his doctor that he was probably reopening a sore that was trying to heal and the sore could simply be caused from constipation. We didn't know what to think but we were thankful that it had finally stopped.

It's amazing when you get older how differently you think. If that happened to my child today, it would be dealt with immediately and I would not accept guessing as an answer. I truly believe I thought if I could just get him home he would be fine.

Content.

Kansas was such a content baby. A little too content, now that I look back. As long as he had his milk, pacifier, and swing we didn't hear anything from him. He would look around and smile. Even when he got up in the night for his feedings he would cry for a few minutes and as soon as my hands touched him he would stop. I also remember Kansas stretching in his sleep and having what would best be described as a tremor all over his body. I thought it was strange but I also thought it was just something different that Kansas did.

It soon got to be very noticeable that Kansas didn't require as much sleep as most babies. Kansas was up many times throughout the night and as long as I was with him he didn't cry. I would just sit there holding him trying to engage him in an infant activity, which can be very limited. I was a stay at home mom so at least I could try to grab a few winks here and there between feedings and my two year old's needs.

I noticed an attachment developing with Kansas, which I would consider unhealthy. The first few months seemed normal. He would smile at people and let them hold him. He loved for his Aunt Angie to put him to sleep but that all eventually changed. He only wanted me. Thankfully my husband, Kris, is a real go-to dad, jumping in there and trying to help with the kids as much as his schedule would allow but the attachment got so extreme, Kansas would not even let his own daddy hold him.

It was so rare for him to be content in someone else's arms. I can actually recall the exact moments when it did occur. When he was about 6 months old on the 4th of July, he laid very still in his Grandma Pfalzgraf's arms just listening to the fireworks. I was not only shocked at this behavior but I was wondering why he didn't bother to look up at the sky. Why wasn't he curious about the loud noise? It was then that I had my first thought that maybe he wasn't hearing well.

After eight months of having a very clingy baby I needed a break. I dropped the kids off at their aunt's and I had a "me" day. (Shopping, getting my hair done and lunch with a friend.) I was gone for about eight hours total and when I returned I learned he had cried the entire time I was gone. I felt horrible. Not only for him but for his aunt. To this day I have guilt from this day wondering if it triggered some type of neurological problem.

Development.

Kansas' physical growth was developing at a normal pace and even ahead of how our daughter had developed. He sat up, crawled, walked and even danced by twelve months. His speech was slow but starting to develop. He could say "Da-Da" and could respond to questions by nodding his head, yes. If we listened real close, we could hear him humming along with the hymns in church.

He was a good eater and would try anything new. His Grandma Rossiter even got him to try a cabbage roll once and he loved it!

There were no concerns with Kansas' physical development and as far as his speech goes we just brushed it off as him being a boy. Our family and friends were telling us boys usually tend to talk later. Also, our daughter talked so much we just figured he couldn't get a word in anyway.

His height and weight were average for his age.

Autism.

January of 2003 I took Kansas for his one-year check-up and MMR vaccination. The pediatrician started to ask all the usual questions. She seemed alarmed and even I didn't like the answers. His vocabulary was limited and I wasn't even sure if he knew what the words meant. He was extremely shy, not looking anyone in the eye. He didn't point at anything like most children do and still wasn't sleeping. When we called his name, he ignored us making us question his hearing. That day was the first time the word AUTISM was brought up. The doctor just said maybe we should check into it in the future and that it was too early to tell.

The drive home was panicky and stressful. I felt so alone and scared. The only AUTISM I knew of was "Rain Man" which is a movie of an autistic man who didn't match up with Kansas at all. I immediately went into denial. "That doctor must be a real quack!" How dare she! I tried to push it out of my mind but couldn't. My husband had the same reaction. "Kansas? AUTISTIC? No way." Instead of checking into it further we stopped talking about it all together. --He's probably just slow because he's a boy. He'll catch up.

Within two months after his first birthday, Kansas became more withdrawn, preferring to be alone. He hated to leave our home and if we had company he would go to another room. He stopped dancing to music and instead would cry and cover his ears. This was very upsetting to Kris and I. Music is extremely important to our family. Kris has a beautiful voice. He is involved with a local band and lead sings every Sunday in church. When Kansas was very small Kris would hold him and sing gospel songs but this too had to come to an end.

All communication was gone. It was replaced with low humming and whining. Tantrums soon became present. My content little baby had transformed into a very stressed little toddler.

Definition of autism according to Webster's dictionary: a mental disorder originating in infancy that is characterized by inability to interact socially, repetitive behavior, and language disorder

Reality.

One night I was home with the kids and Kris was away coaching a basketball game when my parents just happened to drop by. This did not happen very often without a phone call first considering they live an hour away so I knew something was up. They sat me down and handed over information downloaded off of the internet. Oh no, it was that dreaded word again, Autism. As I read down the list of signs to look for, I became ill. Kansas had fourteen out of the eighteen listed:

-Difficulty in expressing needs
-Repeating words in place of normal, responsive language
-Laughing, crying, showing distress for reasons not apparent to others
-Prefers to be alone
-Tantrums
-Difficulty in mixing with others
-May not want to cuddle
-Little or no eye contact
-Unresponsive to normal teaching methods

-Sustained odd play

-Spins objects

-Inappropriate attachments to objects

-Not responsive to verbal cues; acts as if deaf

As I read on looking for a loophole, I started having flashbacks in my head.

-Kansas looking into the air and laughing. When he was about a year old we were sitting in a restaurant and he was staring out the window into a cemetery. He was laughing hysterically. We had no idea what was so funny.

-The new tantrums.

-The cuddling with no one but me.

-The covering of his ears when I would try to read him a book or sing a nursery rhyme.

-The odd play when he would just lay on baby dolls.

-Turning trucks upside down to watch the wheels spin.

-Always wanting to carry a small toy in his hand even if it was just a plastic hippo.

It wasn't easy for my parents to bring this information to my attention and now I had to show it to my husband.

Kris came home and could tell by the look on my face that something was wrong. We went over this description of our child again and again. I believe we were looking for something that jumped off the paper and screamed "No, there isn't anything wrong with your son!"

After a few hours we both decided the time had come and we needed to do everything in our power to help our son.

Help.

Where do we begin? I used to get visits from a program called "Help Me Grow". They help families with children who are birth to 3 years old. They can try and find out answers to any questions you might have. They can monitor the growth and development of your child. I was involved with this program for my daughter but got away from it because there weren't any concerns with her. Now, I needed them. I called them up and what a blessing they turned out to be. I had a home coordinator at my house within a week spending time with Kansas and asking me a zillion questions. Her name was Allison Boggs and after our first visit she soon grew a halo over her head. She woke me up and helped me turn on a light at the end of our tunnel. She also made me see that I wasn't alone. We agreed that Kansas needed early intervention.

An early intervention specialist came to our home by the name of Danielle Greenlee and she would work with him just doing basic tasks like stacking blocks, putting puzzles together or painting. The experience was a real eye opener for me. Kansas was so behind. He wasn't the easiest child to work with either. She couldn't touch him and he seemed to be in his own little world 90% of the time. She would try to get him to complete activities but he would just fall right back into his strange ways of play. I would always be asking Danielle, "What do you think? Do you see signs of autism?" Trying to be professional about it she would say yes and no. I was still searching for someone to say "He's fine."

By this time Kansas was approaching his second birthday and instead of these concerns going away like we wanted, they became more prominent. He also developed some new corky habits. Kansas wanted to stare at the edge of objects like a windowsill or our countertop and walk beside them repeatedly. If you broke up his repetitive cycle he would go into a full blown tantrum. One night he walked around the island in our kitchen staring at the edge of the counter for 1 ½ hrs. We later learned this is called stemming. It is a way for him to release stress and zone out. It actually feels good and soothes him. Not all autistic children stem in the same way. I have witnessed some children with autism stemming by playing with sand or water. Some tend to rock back and forth.

Kansas had an infatuation for skin. Wanting to place his face against it, usually preferring the back of anyone close by. We had to be aware of this in public. Once we were sitting in the bleachers at a basketball game and he pulled up the shirt of a girl in front of us just so he could lay his cheek on her back. Another time we took the kids to the beach and he ran up to a man sunbathing, wrapped both legs around his big belly and laid his face on his chest. Needless to say the man was startled and we were extremely embarrassed. With all of these strange behaviors and lack of progress we were still looking for answers.

I have to admit, I felt somewhat cheated. It's hard for me to accept the fact that there are mothers out there who choose to drink or smoke during pregnancy. I did everything by the book and gave this little child the best start I possibly could yet something is happening to him. I can now look at the situation differently. I know God loves all his children and why wouldn't he give Kansas to us. We are able to love him unconditionally.

Kansas is also blessed by having so many special people in his life. It means so much when an adult puts forth effort into knowing our son. Unfortunately, our society puts people who are different into the strange category and sometimes you can end up being scared to be around them or nervous as to what to say. We are very open about Kansas and have no problem talking about our situation.

We have taken Kansas to Lewisville Church of Christ since he was born and all the members are used to his different corky habits. His bible school teacher, Connie Young, works to teach the little ones and does an excellent job. Kansas really doesn't get too involved in the lessons or so we think. I still believe he is listening even though we question it. A couple who goes to church with us, Dale and Joan Christman, invite us over to their house often. They don't seem to have any problem with Kansas. We were at their house one time and Joan took Kansas out on a paddleboat all by herself. These little efforts mean so much to me. Some of our friends have shied away from us because they just don't know how to handle the situation or know what to say.

Surgery.

When we went in for Kansas' 2 year check-up, his pediatrician still thought it was too early for a diagnosis. I am not a professional but I do know now that it is never too early. The sooner you deal with autism, the better.

The pediatrician informed me that every time we go in for visits, Kansas has fluid on his eardrum and maybe we should find an ENT. I didn't even know what that stood for at the time. --Ear, nose and throat specialist. Immediately I thought that this could be contributing to what seemed to be a hearing loss.

We met with the ENT and he decided that Kansas would benefit from getting tubes put into both ears. This would help the fluid drain and possibly be the answer for why Kansas was not talking. Maybe he just can't hear very clearly. We were hanging on to every possibility.

While we were waiting for surgery day to arrive I took Kansas to my Aunt Diane's house where she just happened to have a train table set up for her grandchildren. Kansas played with that train for our entire visit. It was so exciting to see him have an interest in something and use it in the correct, expected way of play. I went out in search of a train that was age appropriate. I bought him two wooden, magnetic, "Thomas the Tank Engine" cars and had no idea what I had just done. He carried them everywhere. Kansas always felt more secure if he had something in his hands and these were perfect size for his little fists.

April of 2004, Kansas had tubes put in his ears. It was a very scary day for Kris and I. We hated the thought of him having to be put under. After a very short while, I went into the recovery room and saw a very tiny little boy resting peacefully on this big hospital bed. His pacifier vibrating in and out just by habit and his two trains, resting by his head. I was brought right back to his precious innocence and how much I wanted to shield him from today's expected normalcy.

Surgery #2

Unfortunately, the surgery did not improve Kansas' vocabulary. The fluid was now gone but there was no noticeable change in his reaction to sound. Allison wanted us to start with therapy but we needed to get his hearing officially tested first. Kansas couldn't have the basic hearing test that his ENT offered because he wouldn't be able to communicate. We were referred to Morgantown, WV where Kansas could undergo a surgical procedure to identify any hearing problems, if there were any. He would have to be put under again but this time Kris could not come for work reasons so he stayed with our daughter while Kansas, my mom and I started the two-hour trip to Morgantown.

We got to the hospital and Kansas immediately got nervous. He was grinding his teeth and humming. I couldn't blame him. He was not only scared from previous doctor visits and hospitals but also I'm sure he could sense my anxiety. Grandma Rossiter wasn't exactly calm either. We got Kansas pre-registered for the next day, so we were off to a hotel for the night. Staying away from home was not done very often but luckily and surprisingly Kansas did just fine with this adventure. Maybe he liked having his mom and Grandma all to himself.

As soon as we got to the hospital the next morning, they gave him medicine and he fell back asleep. They were able to take him away without screaming and kicking, which was great for all three of us. It wasn't long till the doctor came back to us and said his hearing was fine. It's hard to explain how I felt. Of course, I didn't want my child to have any hearing difficulties but this was a confirmation. Kansas could hear us just fine yet was not learning and developing like a "normal" child. A normal child asks questions and declares their likes and dislikes. A normal child can tell you about their day but my son could not.

Therapy.

Again I turned to my home coordinator from "Help Me Grow". She was able to schedule him with a speech and occupational therapist which was covered through my insurance. I understood the need for a speech therapist but I remember being offended with the mention of an additional therapist. "Why would he need any other kind of therapy?" I guess that was just more denial seeping out of my pores. Also, I honestly did not know what occupational therapy consisted of. An occupational therapist helps the child learn the "jobs" they would normally pick up on their own but haven't. For example, Kansas had never bothered to undress himself. I just always did it for him not knowing that I was causing more harm than good. This is something that would normally come naturally but didn't for Kansas.

Once a week we would make the 1 ½ hour drive and he would receive a combined session of both therapies lasting just an hour. I would sit in for these sessions, which I now know was most likely hindering any progress. He would still have his pacifier through half of the session, crawl into my lap and just hide his face.

I should have left him in that room so they could do their work.

Kansas had a problem with wanting me to carry him all the time. He didn't have the independence issues that most toddlers go through. He would keep getting in front of me with arms up and whining. I dealt with this constantly and even to a more extreme going into these therapy sessions. He did not want to be there.

Guilt. -Driving home after therapies, I would often wonder if Kansas' lack of development was because we couldn't spend the same amount of time with him as we did with our daughter when she was the only child. If you have one child she or he can have all of your attention along with your spouse's. Two kids in the home can be very different. We tried our best but we definitely didn't spend as much time with him individually. I felt tremendous guilt day after day on those long drives home.

The therapy went on at a steady pace and more was brought to my attention that just wasn't right for me to be OK with. Kansas never used silverware when eating. He wouldn't comb his hair or brush his teeth. It seemed like I had to wake up and admit that my child needed special attention.

Surprise!

A beneficial fact I learned right away from his therapists was that Kansas tends to relax when deep pressure is applied to his joints. So instead of gently touching him they would hold onto him tightly or press down on his shoulders with heaviness. To my surprise it was easy to recognize Kansas felt at ease when this was done. We started using this method at home and church which proved to be very beneficial.

I soon found out that Kansas could count. I was amazed when the speech therapist would just say "one" and he would take off counting to a different number each time. We weren't sure how high he could go. The occupational therapist had him matching colors within no time. Kansas was turning into our exciting little bundle of mystery.

I do believe I learned a lot from the pediatric therapy unit at Marietta Memorial Hospital but if I only knew how much more progress we were going to be making in the future, I wouldn't have believed it.

Brushing.

Eventually, it seemed like we had reached a brick wall with the therapy at Marietta. His occupational therapist decided to begin what is called the "brushing" technique. The technical name was *Deep Tactile Pressure*. It was supposed to help Kansas feel centered and be calming for him. It started out very intense. I would use this little plastic brush with very soft bristles and rub it on his skin. I had to press firmly and do his arms, hands, legs, feet and back. After brushing I would then compress his joints. We had to do this every 90 minutes for two weeks and the sessions would get farther and farther apart. This was experimental to see how Kansas would react to it and if it would help him focus or calm his nerves. I honestly can't say if it helped. I know he didn't like it at first but then grew to enjoy it. Sometimes he would bring me the brush when it wasn't even time. We didn't see any major change and the interest from him faded so we ended up stopping it all together.

These unusual techniques seem so strange until you have a child who might benefit from them. I was willing to do anything that brought my child out of his shell.

Finality.

The "Help Me Grow" coordinator wanted to know when we would like to get an official diagnosis for Kansas. The harsh reality of admitting it was still too much for my husband and I. We just kept putting it off. Finally we agreed to get this done and we scheduled Kansas for an evaluation with a group of doctors from Ohio State University. They were holding an all day clinic in Athens, Ohio.

Kris, Kansas and I had to be there early in the morning and of course living out in nowhere we again had to drive a couple of hours. Kansas was put through many tests that included playing with toys, reacting to sounds, and physical analysis.

During the lunch break, we went into a little room that happened to have many drawers. He couldn't stand it. Instead of eating he chose to pull out each drawer to the same exact length. He even stood there and lined them all up by looking across the top of each drawer. I noticed that no one else sitting in the room thought this behavior was strange. They were all there for the same reasons we were. They were questioning their own child's development. Why is this happening to our children? Why is it so prevalent in our area. We live near the Ohio river and I do wonder if that has something to do with it. Is it in the water? Is it in the air? Will we ever know?

We were asked many questions and by the end of the day we were all three exhausted. About a week later I received a packet in the mail with the very first paper reading in bold letters:

Diagnosis: Autism and Global Development Delay

I just sat down and cried. I guess it was the finality of it. There was no longer a question. My son had autism.

Preschool.

The "Help Me Grow" coordinator was not through with us yet. She had talked us into enrolling Kansas into preschool, which happened to be free since he had a diagnosis. This was a hard decision. He was so attached to me and I pictured him crying everyday when I dropped him off. He was still very attached to his pacifier as well and he would not be able to take it to school with him so this whole idea seemed impossible.

He started two weeks before his third birthday and I was terrified. Of course, he was scared to death and was screaming just as hard when I picked him up as when I dropped him off which happened to only be 2 ½ hours. It felt like a lifetime to me and I didn't even leave the parking lot. As I was putting him back in the truck to go home, he was shaking and the tears were flowing like a faucet. I wondered how Kansas and I could possibly go through this every day. The next day I forced myself through the same process and got the same result. I needed major support from my husband.

Kris hated the thought of Kansas stressing so bad but he did remind me that older children go through this as well when they start kindergarten. It was our first time to separate and it wasn't going to be easy. We did actually talk about holding off until he was older. Thank goodness, we decided to give it a little more time and I am now so grateful that we did not pull him out. The next day Kansas seemed to be in good spirits and did much better. By just one week after starting he actually was smiling when I left and was participating in classroom activities. I couldn't believe it! The future looked so much brighter. --I did eventually leave the parking lot.

Involved.

Preschool turned out to be such a blessing. His teacher, Jacci Morgan, seemed to know exactly how to get through to Kansas and we immediately saw improvement with independence, comprehension, and consistency. Kansas started receiving his therapy through the school system and it was provided during preschool hours so I no longer had to make the long trips for his weekly sessions. We also added physical therapy to his agenda. Again, I resisted adding more therapy thinking he did not need it but was persuaded by the physical therapist, Rachel Perkins, and I'm so glad she talked me into it. The more we involved Kansas, the more he improved. One night when I was in the kitchen doing dishes I heard Kansas humming which was not new but this time was different. As I listened more closely I could recognize a tune. I was so thrilled. I just stood there hoping he would never stop. Luckily, he did it again when Kris was home. We just sat there with big grins on both of our faces. I talked to his teacher about it the next day and it turns out it's the song they sing every day to begin "circle time". I was beyond words. Not only is he listening, but he was enjoying music again.

Kansas was also showing problem solving skills in addition to exercising more independence. His occupational therapist, Lea Ladiga, was teaching him basic toddler "jobs" and it was coming along slowly but surely. He was starting to show interest in putting his own shoes on and zipping his own jacket. These little things mean the world to me and most people don't even think about their kids achieving such a simple task.

We came home from church on a Wednesday night and Kris and I immediately began our nightly ritual of getting everyone ready for bed when I noticed Kansas had his pacifier in his mouth. At that time we were trying to break him from the habit so I couldn't figure out how he got it. I went to the kitchen and there was a chair pulled up to the "binky cupboard" Climbing is normal for most children but not my Kansas. I was thrilled.

He was starting to show us more personality too. I left him with Grandma Rossiter for just 20 minutes one day and when I got back she had him marching all over the house with a big grin. Needless to say we then marched everywhere even if it was just to brush our teeth. One time in bible study he needed to place star stickers on a piece of paper and as all the other children took each star off individually, Kansas peels off the back of the entire sticker card and puts the whole thing on his paper with one motion. I couldn't argue with that. He did put the stars on the paper like I asked.

Kansas wasn't speaking so he came up with other ways of communicating. If he wanted my attention when I was doing dishes, he would bring me a dry dishtowel because he knew that was my next step to finish. I needed to dry my hands. If he needed deep pressure, he would take my hand and push it into his chin. The progress was in full bore.

His speech therapy was given to him by Megan Sherman and I think he had a crush on her. Anytime I mentioned Miss Megan to him he would grin real big and get excited. We even took him for speech lessons through the summer and he had no problem giving her an hour of his day. She did a great job and even had him using some sign language such as the signs for more, thank you and no. This is a good example of people in his life going out of their way to help. Megan did not have to give him summer lessons but did.

Walt Disney World.

Kansas had about four months of school and then it was summer break. I didn't want the progress to stop so I went through some slight panic. The only thing that was offered in our area was a camp that he would attend once a week and he would be with a large group of kids but still working with the teachers and therapists he was used to. I also signed him up for a private class of gymnastics once a week but he still needed more. We did see some regression such as interest and focusing.

That same summer we took the kids to Walt Disney World. My husband refused to fly so we started our 16-hour drive from Ohio to Florida. We left at 10:00pm thinking the kids would sleep most of the trip. "What were we thinking?" Kansas was still up at 4:00am but he was so happy just sitting in the back with a big grin on his face. Maybe he could feel the anticipation from the rest of us.

When we got to Florida we decided to stay on the beach for a couple of days. Kansas loved the beach but was a little frightened of the water chasing him up onto the sand. We then spent a week at Disney and I feared how Kansas would react to being away from home for so long. To my surprise he never let out a peep the entire vacation. Disney was everything we dreamed of and more. Kansas loved all the rides, the fireworks, the food and even the big characters walking around the parks. He even gave Mickey Mouse a high five. We should have known his most favorite part of the visit would be when we rode the monorail. Sometimes we would just get on to rest and let Kansas zone out for a few minutes.

As we drove back home I just reflected on how much we all truly relaxed and promised myself that I would not stress anymore about leaving home with Kansas. He couldn't express to me anything about our vacation but he didn't have to. I could see it in his eyes. We will be going on many trips in the future and we will go back to Disney for sure.

To this day Kansas thrives on vacations. I don't get it but I'll go with it. We take a vacation every summer and it does all of us wonders as a family.

Here we go again.

Preschool started in September and again, I was nervous. The very first day, Kansas let go of my hand and ran right into the school. That went better than what I was expecting. I really don't believe he forgets anything.

Everyday I would arrive a little bit early to pick him up so that I could spy on him interacting with his peers. There wasn't much contact with the other kids but he did participate in most of the activities.

I did notice this constant humming coming from him when his preschool time was almost up. I believe it was his nerves and maybe just from being so tired. Also since Kansas was not getting his pacifier as much, he began the annoying habit of grinding his teeth. I actually wanted to give it back to him so we wouldn't have to hear it.

We were trying to break him of his pacifier completely but he would come home and be so tired he would go directly to the "pacifier cupboard" and state the word "binky". With very few words in Kansas' vocabulary he knew if he said it, he would receive it.

Eventually, we ended up giving the binky to him just at night. When he started losing his teeth we eliminated it all together. It was a fight every night for about 2 weeks but he got over it just like any other kid.

DAN!

I was talking to a friend one day and she asks me if I had ever heard of DAN!. I had no clue what she was talking about. She read in a magazine where there are doctors out there who are treating autism with diet and supplements and were getting great results from it. DAN! Stands for Defeat Autism Now. Needless to say I was very interested.

I started making phone calls and eventually found some information on the internet. I decided to make an appointment with a DAN! doctor in Cleveland. A four hour adventure and again he was put through so much. They tested his urine, hair and blood. They then asked me questions that could help them decide what would be best for Kansas. They immediately wanted me to put him on vitamins and supplements. They even handed me a crème that they claimed would pull out any toxins that might be present in Kansas' body. A side effect from the crème was an odor of skunk. I couldn't believe what I was hearing. We ended up taking 13 different vitamins home and a doctor's visit that cost us almost $800.00. I wondered how we would be able to afford this and how does other families with autism pay for such medical needs.

Now, how do we get him to take a vitamin? He of course was not interested. I was able to crush up most of them and open capsules so that I could put it in his juice without him knowing. It took me weeks to get into a rhythm. The cream was scary. I didn't want my son to stink. I put it on him reluctantly. We could eventually smell something but it was very light and didn't get strong unless he would sweat. The smell lasted about two months. I called the doctor to see why the smell went away and delightfully I was told he must not have any toxins left to remove. I went to our regular pediatrician to have him checked and not only the bad metals were removed but also the cream had lowered his iron. So now I was having to give him an additional supplement of iron.

We went back to the DAN! Doctor 6 weeks after our first visit and got the result from all the tests they took. They told me Kansas cannot digest dairy and should have it removed from his diet. They also wanted me to remove wheat even though they didn't see any signs of it being harmful to him. They informed me that this was all experimental and all kids are different but they do get good results from this type of a diet with most of the autistic children that they see. As far as metals being in his system at the time of testing his amount of aluminum was extremely high.

The metals are very overwhelming to me. We are always in search of a cause for this disease and we have heard many opinions. Kansas received all of his vaccines on time so we do question if maybe his immune system needed a different shot recipe than other children. There is also the fact that we live 6 miles from the Ohio river where there are many plants putting chemicals into the air and one of them just happens to be a plant that makes aluminum. It's very scary to think we might have caused this to happen to our son just by getting his shots or living in the wrong place. I wonder if we will ever know.

Kris and I decided after receiving these test results that we would give this clinic 1 year and if Kansas had a remarkable reaction to any of their methods we would stick with it. This was all very expensive and truly we did not know how we were going to afford it but we just had to give it a try. After much paperwork was exchanged back and forth with our insurance, they did start paying for the vitamins. We still had to pay for the doctor visits and that was enough.

We put Kansas on the casein free- gluten free diet. (milk free- wheat free) It was the hardest thing I ever had to do. Kansas had a very good appetite and up to that point would eat pretty much anything I put in front of him but it was still hard just realizing how much food on the market has milk or wheat or even both. Then we had the trouble of eating at family's homes or out and about and sticking to such a strict diet. It was hard but we did it. We gave it a good chance sticking to the diet for a year and a ½ but it just didn't help Kansas. We stuck to it for so long because we had built up so much hope hearing how well it worked for other children. I noticed more progress if we just watched his sugar intake and stayed with healthy foods. The supplements and vitamins were fine but again we didn't notice remarkable changes happening.

I hear these methods of doctoring can be very beneficial for some children but not all.

Kris found a news article where a family was having success using a vitamin called Sonic Cholesterol. This article read that some children with autism have a low cholesterol count and benefited from taking this vitamin. I looked into it further and the first step we needed to take was getting his cholesterol tested. All these tests he had been given and this one was not done. Well I did not want to drive clear back to Cleveland so I called my regular family doctor to see if they would test him. They had no problem doing this for me and as it turns out his cholesterol was low. With the help of Charles DeNunzio Jr. DO and Samantha Farnesworth PAC I was able to get Sonic Cholesterol for my son. We didn't notice anything for a while but after about 3 months we could say he was much calmer. We get this off the internet with our doctors prescription.

We truly believe it was Sonic Cholesterol that calmed our son enough to sit through church. Church is very important to us and raising our children in the church is absolutely necessary. Kansas would cry as soon as we pulled into the parking lot. He would cry when we sung hymns and cover his ears. He would throw things if the service lasted too long. Now he still isn't thrilled about being there but his reaction to the whole process is much more acceptable. During the last prayer on a Sunday night instead of screaming and throwing a toy he simply yelled out "Say Amen!" Could you really get mad at that? It gave everyone a good laugh.

A bad habit that ended was him hitting his head. When Kansas got to big to throw himself down on the floor for a full blown tantrum he began hitting himself in the forehead. This was so disturbing. About three months after administering this supplement the hitting had stopped.

Kansas always hated getting a hair cut. We always go to the same barber, Noel McFarland, and he is another angel that goes out of his way to accommodate my son. I will always be grateful for the patience and understanding we receive from Noel. It's been a process but now we can go right in and Kansas has no problem with it.

Spongebob Squarepants.

Kansas finished his first full year of preschool. He did so well and improved all the time. The little things mean so much when it comes to understanding autism. Just hearing him say words that were somewhat recognizable was huge. We were sitting on the couch and Kansas recited a line from the cartoon Spongebob Squarepants. I asked Kris to come in and listen. He said the line over and over again and we were able to recognize it. The excitement of watching his mouth form these words was indescribable. Now we know the ability is there.

If only I could have a conversation with my son.

My husband always said, "Wonder what he is thinking."

Kansas has other favorite cartoon characters. He loves Charlie Brown. Every once in a while we will hear him say "Good Grief!" He sometimes acts out movie scenes such as Dash from The Incredibles running around the table reciting his exact same lines. When he does these things we just look at it as a game and try to figure out what scene he is acting out now.

He loves to make the same noises as on TV. If there is going to be a loud noise then he is going to make that same loud noise at the same time. Maybe when he grows up he can be the one who adds sound to picture.

A.B.A.

A little boy by the name of Christian who was the same age as Kansas and was also diagnosed with autism lived nearby. I was interested in what all his parents were doing as far as education. I called his mother Tiffany and that was the first time I learned about Applied Behavioral Analysis. ABA was really helping her son and so I wanted to check into it. ABA is a very intense one on one method of teaching. They basically teach in detail for a reward. For instance, they might lay three items on the table and say, "Give me the ball." When the child does this he could receive a piece of his favorite food or a favorite toy. Everything sounded good to my husband and I but we did have a problem dealing with him only being four years old and having full days of constant interaction. It didn't take long for everyone around Kansas to inform us that this is exactly what he needed. Another transition not only for him but for us too. I began wondering whom it was harder on.

Kris fixed up a room in our basement and we met the two women who would be overseeing our own ABA therapist. Kari Marx and Cindy Robertson came into our home and got it all ready to go. I could tell from the beginning that these two knew what they were doing. I learned that they both had autistic children of their own and they were now active in normal society. This got me very excited. Our school system provided our ABA therapist, Carol Marmie. She started the summer of 2006. The results were amazing. The first day she worked with him she got him to go potty. For a reward he would receive half of a fruit chew. That's all it takes? He hadn't gone to the potty for me in months. Within days he went from handing her objects as she named them to actually reciting their names himself. (ball, book, toothbrush, etc.)

He soon started saying "Thank you" when we would hand him something and he was now pointing instead of standing in front of objects and grunting. We still had to say what the object was but he would then repeat us. Saying the word just like he had been talking since birth. This was amazing. We couldn't believe he was talking and here he was repeating any word we threw at him.

We were lucky enough to have a therapist who we liked and trusted. She would take him swimming with other children and that would give him the opportunity to interact with his peers but also work on sensory issues like dealing with the water and different temperatures. Being wet or even walking with bare feet on cement can be difficult for children with autism. He went from clinging onto her to eventually going down the slide and swimming away on his own. This whole process was also developing some much needed independence.

One of our goals for Kansas was to identify family members from pictures and eventually by seeing them in person. It didn't take long before we were able to point to someone and ask Kansas, "Who is that?" He would then state "mommy", "daddy", or "Grandpa Rossiter". I believe this was also helping him not be so distant with family as well.

His therapist or aide, Carol, was with him everyday the next school year. She would work with him for half a day using the ABA method and then he would go to preschool in the afternoon. Everything was going great and we were seeing progress. I was so thankful for everyone involved in this little guy's life and I could tell they all truly cared. Everyone who gets involved with Kansas seems to love being around him. Carol stayed with Kansas throughout the next summer but then broke the scary news to us that she had to move on for job security. I was scared to death. A new aide? Oh no, panic. What if we get some crazy person or someone who does not understand autism?

Fulfilling our greatest fears, his next aide did not work out. She was new to the ABA method and we soon noticed she was bending the rules. It wasn't long before she had to switch to another child because she wasn't physically able to keep up with Kansas. She actually lost him one day and he was 2 blocks away!

We were then introduced to Windi Piatt. I was excited right from the first day, once I saw she was young and agile. Kansas seemed to hit it off with Windi right away. She was new to the ABA method as well, but jumped on board and was willing to learn. She had it down in no time. Kansas was progressing again.

Kansas was now sleeping better. He still had trouble getting to sleep but once he was down he would sleep all night. I believe this came because we were now stimulating his brain. He was now occupied enough to actually get exhausted.

We were getting more brave about leaving Kansas with babysitters and were even getting teenagers to come in for the evening every once in a while. He was fine with this and I think enjoyed it.

Potty training.

Kansas was now 5 years old and was still not showing an interest in using the bathroom. He would go for his teachers and aide but only for a reward. This was hard for Kris and I to deal with. We had to show great patience. He was so big and wearing a size 6 diaper. We had been taking him to the toilet since he was 3 just trying to do our part in the training. I know they did the same at school. He was not a least bit interested until 3 months before his 6th birthday. I was in the kitchen and I heard water running. Kansas liked to play with the faucets so this was not a new noise but I went to check on him anyway. I couldn't believe my eyes. He was standing there completely naked and peeing in the toilet. I sat down right there and cried. My boy was not only using the toilet correctly but he did it all by himself. I was in shock. I praised him again and again with hugs and kisses. We rolled on the floor and wrestled because he loves to do that. His dad came home and had the same reaction once I convinced him I was not joking. We called all the family to share the news.

Kansas never wore a diaper again. I was finally able to put big boy underwear on him and he seemed to really like them. He never had an accident except for maybe two different times in the night. I guess all those years of sighing and dragging him into the restroom going through all the motions of using the bathroom finally paid off. Don't think we didn't get lazy sometimes and just not fool with it. We are human and we did take some breaks on the training but with all the time that someone was taking him to the bathroom he was actually paying attention. Who knew?

Today he has no trouble with bathroom needs at school but at home he gets too comfortable and sometimes comes out of the bathroom without pulling his pants up. He sometimes wants to touch his poop and we still don't know why that is. We just tell him "no" and try not to make a big deal about it, making sure he washes his hands real good.

Peers.

Kansas' preschool classroom was limited. There weren't many children who were considered "typical", meaning no neurological or physical problems. We were encouraged by the ABA coordinator to change schools and give him more exposure to "typical" children. We talked it over and decided to give it a try. This transition proved to be very beneficial. He was using more words and taking turns. He had exposure to different teachers and he seemed to form a bond with another little boy. I would wake him up and tell him "Time for school. Let's go see Miss Windi" and he would then say "David?". He was verifying that he was going to go see his new little friend. It was so exciting.

Kansas learned so much this year. He was at full speed. He was coming to us with more words. We still didn't get sentences from him but I truly believe it will come in time. He can sing an entire song with no hesitation so I know the ability is there. He still chooses not to talk unless he has to. One time I was driving to close to the person in front of me and when they turned off the road I almost hit them. Kansas yells, "Look out!" He sees no need to talk unless necessary.

Blessings.

If autism has touched your life in some way, it is not a burden or plague. It is a blessing and honor for you to embrace. The Lord has special children to share with this world and He is trusting you with his prized possessions. Whether you are a parent, relative, friend of the family, or even a neighbor please go out of your way to be involved in this child's life. It is worth every second and instead of fixing the child you discover yourself.

Now.

Kansas is 6 years old now. Our journey is not near over and it never will be. Not because he has autism but because he is our son. You always want the best for your kids and we will be there every step of the way for all 3 of ours. Yes, I said 3. We had another child 3 years after having Kansas. It was a girl and she never showed any signs of autism but you better believe I have taken all precautions and put her on a different shot recipe. She never received more than one shot a month and didn't get her MMR until she was three years old. The medical field can tell me all they want and I do believe vaccines are necessary but I have not been shown proof that they didn't harm my child. Kansas received his booster shots for school one at a time over a period of whole year. By doing this with him and my third child, there were no side effects and it was a lot less stress.

The children now all thrive off of one another just like any other siblings. Our oldest being the example and the smallest being the little terror. Kansas learns a lot from both of his sisters but also teaches them a great deal. As for me and Kris' relationship, it could not be stronger. Unfortunately, when a couple has to deal with so many emotions all at once it's hard for them to make it last. We have been through so much together and I couldn't imagine it any other way.

Kansas is not only comfortable with his immediate family but he also loves his extended family as well. He enjoys excavating with Grandpa and wrestling with his cousins.

Kansas is in Kindergarten. I believe the symptoms of autism can be lessened by integrating these children into a regular classroom environment. We have placed Kansas in a public school, a typical classroom with a personal aide. He is receiving special one on one education on the side plus all his therapies. We did receive resistance from our school system by choosing this route but he is doing fine and thriving. We were blessed with a teacher, Crystal Longwell, who goes out of her way to accommodate each child in her classroom. His new aide, Terrie Isaly, is wonderful. He is so happy and content with both of them. I was much more calm about this huge transition from preschool to school-age because one important lesson I have learned over the past 6 years is to not worry so much about Kansas but to have more faith in him and his abilities. God will not give you anything you cannot handle. Our family is a true example of that phrase.

Insert from my husband Kris:

It's very difficult to express in words the thoughts of Autism as a father. Being raised with a loving family that were all so educated and well versed in the "gift of gab", I never dreamed I'd have a son who struggled with normal communication skills. I'm sure I went through all the normal behaviors of a father. I first was in denial. Isn't that so typical of a man. I hoped and often prayed for it to just go away, but it didn't go away and the problem needed to be dealt with. As much as I recall even after we had Kansas diagnosed I still was hoping he would somehow snap out of it. What to do? Deal with it. Work through it just as I'd done any problem in life. Find a way to fix the problem. But wait! There is no set rule to follow. Every autistic child is different. I don't care what the doctors say or any professional child psychologist has to say on the matter, no autistic child is the same and no "Special Treatment" is going to be the quick fix for your child. After I came to grips with the fact that my son needed help we would have tried anything to improve his condition. We tried vitamins, diets, went to doctors who specialize in autism, pills, schooling, you name it.

I've come to look at autism as not a handicap as some would like to refer to it as, but instead I look at it as a disease that has and can be cured. You don't know how many times I have wanted to blame someone for this happening to my son. I've blamed the "shot". I've blamed the factory down the road. I've second-guessed myself for something I may have done, but the problem would still be here no matter who I blamed. I've come to realize that this is a situation that is a part of maturity in life. God has sent this child for *me* to grow. Not just emotionally or spiritually, but he has taught me how to be a more patient and loving father. With all due respect to my father, he wasn't very patient with us kids at home growing up. My mother once told me I acted just like him, and watching him through the years I never understood why he would get angry at the little things in life. Such as spilling milk at the dinner table or running and jumping in the house. All of which were never acceptable in our home. But as I have raised my children I've learned to be more patient with all my kids because of learning how to deal with autism. What doesn't kill you makes you stronger. God will never give you more than you can bear. If life gives you lemons make lemonade. You get the picture. Every cloud has a silver lining.

You come to appreciate more things with an autistic child. My son has different tendencies than some children with autism. He likes affection and love. He often gives hugs and sits on your lap, but don't let that fool you, he likes it because it's a way to stem. He likes the feel of skin and he also likes deep pressure. This combination has him sitting against you a lot and although plenty of people will tell you stemming is bad (which it can be) this happens to be quite nice to love on him and get in your own affection. You often see the world a little different than some people get to see it, through the eyes of your autistic child. The way my son sees things makes me want to look harder so I can see them too. There sure is a lot of guessing sometimes because you don't always see what he is seeing. Then again he may show you the world is still amazing.

The one thing we all need to remember is that every person in this world is different, so why does that make autistic children that odd? Funny thing is Kansas' Grandpa likes to be with him because they see things the same way and like to do the same things. Does that make Grandpa autistic or strange? No, because Grandpa understands how to communicate. My wife says it best. That little thing in your brain that lets you talk to people just doesn't work quite right in our little boy, but we still love him.

When you get upset when you've had a bad day because your child isn't progressing the way you wish he or she would, just remember there are a lot worse things than autism. I can't imagine not having my son the way he is. It is "his" personality. He is the way he is and that's how we will accept him. Picture your autistic child not in your life at all and you will not be so depressed about it. It can be a blessing not a curse. There will be days when you are so discouraged and you probably will cry, but you will also have days when you'll be somewhere shopping or on the go and you will see a so called "normal" child and you will be so glad for the blessing that has been given to you.

Do your best every day and lean on the rest of your family. Your spouse is the most important person in your life so vent when needed and let them do the same. Last I heard the divorce rate for parents raising an autistic child was somewhere in the 75% range. If anything autism has brought our family closer. I can't imagine single parents dealing with autism on their own.

Life is a challenge so live everyday to better yourself and your family. Most importantly pray to God for guidance. Remember to cherish the blessing that has been given to you.

Interview with Kansas' big sister who is 8 years old:

Describe autism.
Karigan: Autism is where you can't speak for a little bit and you have trouble telling people what you want.

Do you believe Kansas is improving?
Karigan: Yes, I do.

What do you like about him now compared to a few years ago?
Karigan: That he really likes to hug me and let's me kiss him on the cheek.

Do you ever get embarrassed when you are with Kansas?
Karigan: No.

What do you think Kansas will be when he grows up?
Karigan: A train engineer or a drummer.

If you had one wish for Kansas what would it be?
Karigan: That he will pass each grade in school.

www.ingramcontent.com/pod-product-compliance
Lightning Source LLC
Chambersburg PA
CBHW021232280526
45784CB00005B/2073